QLD
QUEENSLAND
SA
SOUTH AUSTRALIA
NSW
NEW SOUTH WALES
ACT
AUSTRALIAN CAPITAL TERRITORY
VIC
VICTORIA
TAS
TASMANIA
N
W
E
S
AF584863

KYLE SURRY

KIDS' GUIDE
TO
AUSTRALIA'S
STATES & TERRITORIES
DISCOVERING
NSW
NEW
SOUTH
WALES
REDBACK
publishing

First Published 2026 by
Redback Publishing
Suite 6, 13a Narabang Way,
Belrose NSW 2085
Australia

www.redbackpublishing.com
orders@redbackpublishing.com

ISBN 978-1-761400-61-2

Author: Kyle Surry
Editors: Lucinda Dodds and Emma Dobinson
Designer: Redback Publishing

Original illustrations © Redback Publishing 2026
Originated by Redback Publishing

MIX
Paper from responsible sources
FSC www.fsc.org FSC™ C001507

Acknowledgements
Abbreviations: l—left, r—right, b—bottom, t—top, c—centre, m—middle
We would like to thank the following for permission to reproduce photographs: (Images © shutterstock, Alamy) p8-9 - E. Le Bihan - http://www.acmssearch.sl.nsw.gov.au/search/itemDetailPaged.cgi?itemID=845003, Public Domain, https://commons.wikimedia.org/w/index.php?curid=29765211, p9rc - Gosse, Thomas, 1765-1844 - https://nla.gov.au/nla.obj-135292038/view, Public Domain, https://commons.wikimedia.org/w/index.php?curid=97271767, p15bl - Harley Kingston / Shutterstock.com, p18-19 - mastersky / Shutterstock.com, p29tc - Squiresy92 with elements adapted from Sodacan - Own work, Public Domain, https://commons.wikimedia.org/w/index.php?curid=43995590, p32b - ArliftAtoz2205 / Shutterstock.com

NATIONAL LIBRARY OF AUSTRALIA
A catalogue record for this book is available from the National Library of Australia

CONTENTS

Bondi Beach

A LONG TIME AGO

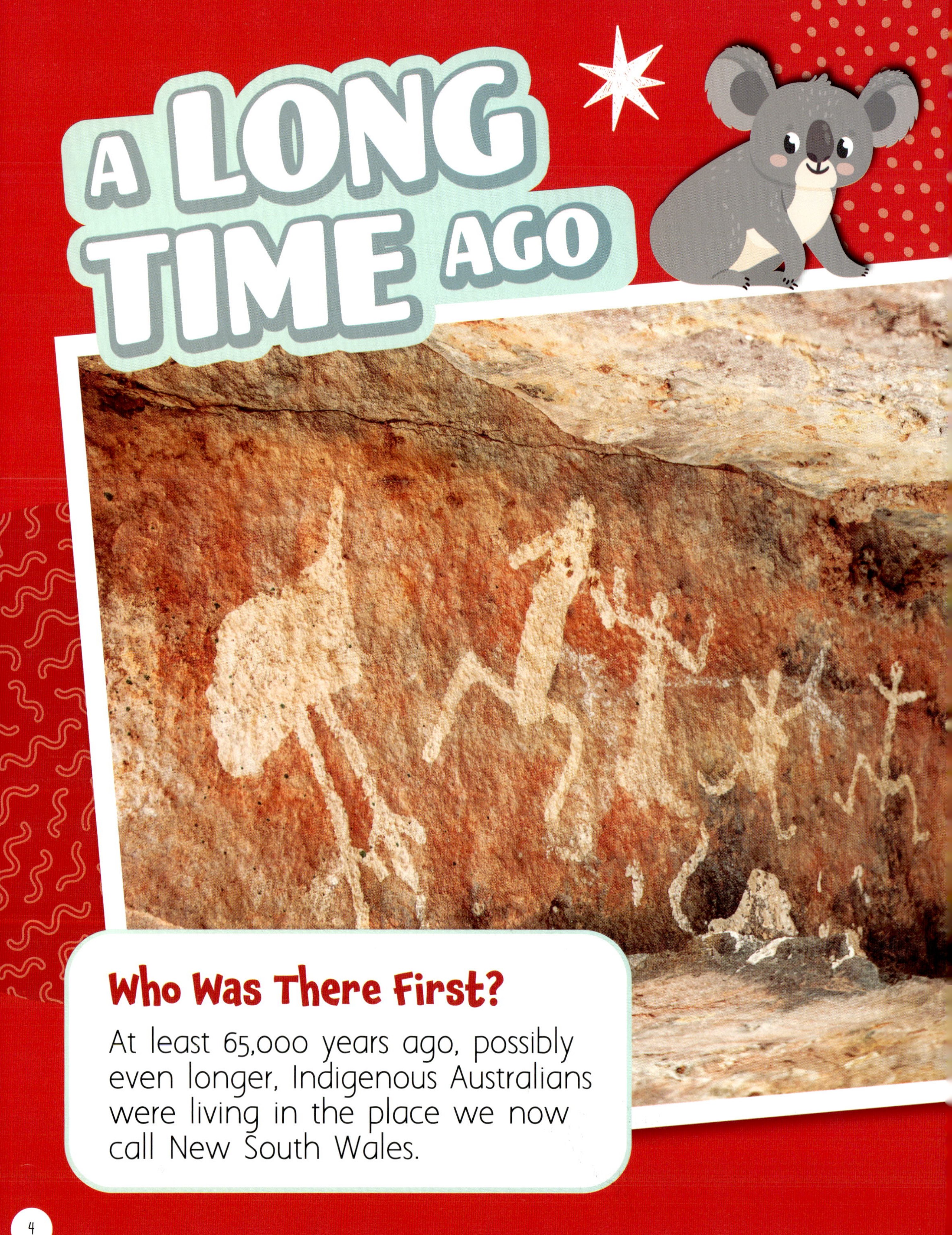

Who Was There First?

At least 65,000 years ago, possibly even longer, Indigenous Australians were living in the place we now call New South Wales.

Indigenous nations of the Sydney area:
• Eora • Dharawal
• Dharug • Guringai
The Wiradjuri nation covers a very large area of New South Wales.
Wiradjuri
There are many Indigenous nations across the state of NSW.
Gundabooka National Park

ANCIENT LANDSCAPES

Most of New South Wales is very different from what it used to be like long ago. Despite this, we can still find parts of it that look like they did hundreds or even thousands of years in the past.

Lake Mungo

This lake is dry now, but it was once an area where Indigenous Australians could hunt, fish and gather food. Ancestors were living in the area over 65,000 years ago.

Wollemi pine

Blue Mountains

This is a rugged region of mountains and hidden valleys. In one of these valleys lives the ancient Wollemi pine. This type of tree has been around for millions of years, ever since the dinosaurs were alive.

Lake Mungo

Farms across New South Wales have replaced the forests and grasslands that were there before settlers arrived over 200 years ago.

THE CONVICTS ARRIVE

In 1788, over a thousand people from Britain arrived in New South Wales. Most of them were convicts.

Australia Day

The convicts and their guards went ashore at what is now Sydney. They landed on 26 January, 1788. This is the date we now call Australia Day.

The convicts were sent far away from Britain as a punishment for committing crimes.

It took eight months for them to sail from Britain to New South Wales. These eleven ships are called the First Fleet.

Indigenous Australians were not happy that strangers from overseas were settling on their lands.

WHERE IS NEW SOUTH WALES?

New South Wales is in the southeast of Australia. It is one of the eight states and territories of Australia, and it is the fourth largest state by area. Its shortened name is written as NSW.

Where are the borders of New South Wales?

HOW MANY PEOPLE?

There are more people in New South Wales than in any other state or territory of Australia. One out of every three Australians lives in NSW.

People from many countries around the world have settled in NSW. In the past, most of the migrants came from the UK. Today, India, China and New Zealand are some of the main countries of origin for migrants to NSW.

Almost one out of every three people in NSW was born overseas.

NSW has over 8.5 million people!

THE BIGGEST CITIES

Sydney

- Sydney is the capital city of NSW
- Sydney is on the east coast of Australia, near the beaches and the Pacific Ocean
- About two out of every three people in NSW live in Sydney
- There are over 5.5 million people in Sydney

Newcastle

- The second largest city in NSW
- It is on the east coast, north of Sydney
- Newcastle is a port city
- Coal is one of Newcastle's main exports
- There are about half a million people in Newcastle and the regions nearby

Wollongong

- The third largest city in NSW
- It is on the east coast, south of Sydney
- Wollongong is an industrial centre and a port city
- There are over 300,000 people in Wollongong and the regions nearby

THE LAND

New South Wales has a long range of mountains running all the way down its eastern side. They are called the Great Dividing Range.

These mountains play an important part in making the western part of NSW much dryer than it is along the coast. The mountains stop a lot of the water in the air reaching inland from the ocean and then falling as rain.

Temperatures have been recorded in NSW ranging from -23°C up to 50°C.

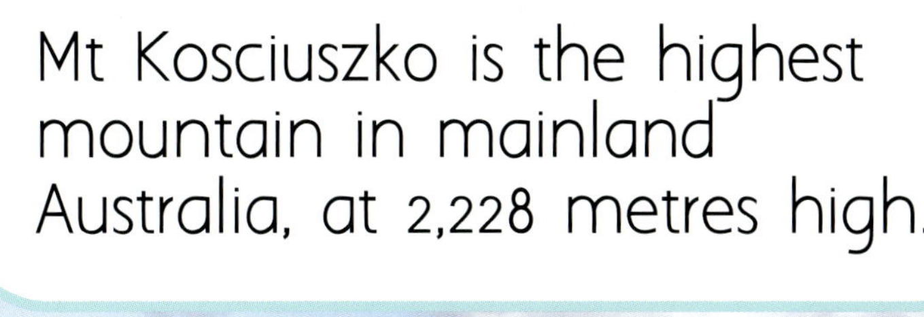

Mt Kosciuszko is the highest mountain in mainland Australia, at 2,228 metres high.

Mount Kosciuszko

There are rainforests in some parts of NSW, but there are also hot, arid areas in the west.

Great Dividing Range

RIVERS THAT FLOOD

The rivers in New South Wales can be dry one year, and then full of flooding water the next.

These rivers were once important for the transport of settlers and their farm produce. Paddle steamers used the Murray River to carry most of the wool produced in the area to larger towns where it was sold.

Biggest Rivers in New South Wales

- The Darling
- The Murray
- The Murrumbidgee
- The Lachlan
- The Macquarie
- The Namoi
- The Hawkesbury
- The Hunter
- The Macleay
- The Clarence
- The Shoalhaven

Darling River

Most of the water used in NSW for homes and agriculture comes from rivers, but also from bores that access underground sources of water.

Paddle steamer on the Murray River

GROWING FOOD

Agriculture is a major industry in New South Wales, producing food for local use, and for export to other states of Australia and to countries around the world. The control of pests and diseases of plants and animals is very important for the food growers of NSW.

Coastal Lowlands

The coastal lowlands on the eastern coast feature many beautiful lakes and beaches. The area has fertile soil for farming, and it is also the most densely populated area in the state.

Western Plains

The western plains form two thirds of NSW. They have low rainfall and sparse vegetation. Using careful water control, farmers use this area for crops such as wheat, barley and rice. They also raise sheep and cattle for meat and dairy products.

COAL MINES

Coal mining is still one of the most important industries in New South Wales.

The local coal mines produce millions of tonnes of coal each year. This coal is used to generate electricity locally. It is also exported to a number of countries, including Japan, China and South Korea.

A large part of the carbon dioxide pollution in NSW comes from burning coal to make electricity. Much of the electricity produced in NSW comes from burning coal.

Carbon dioxide is a greenhouse gas.

STATE GOVERNMENT

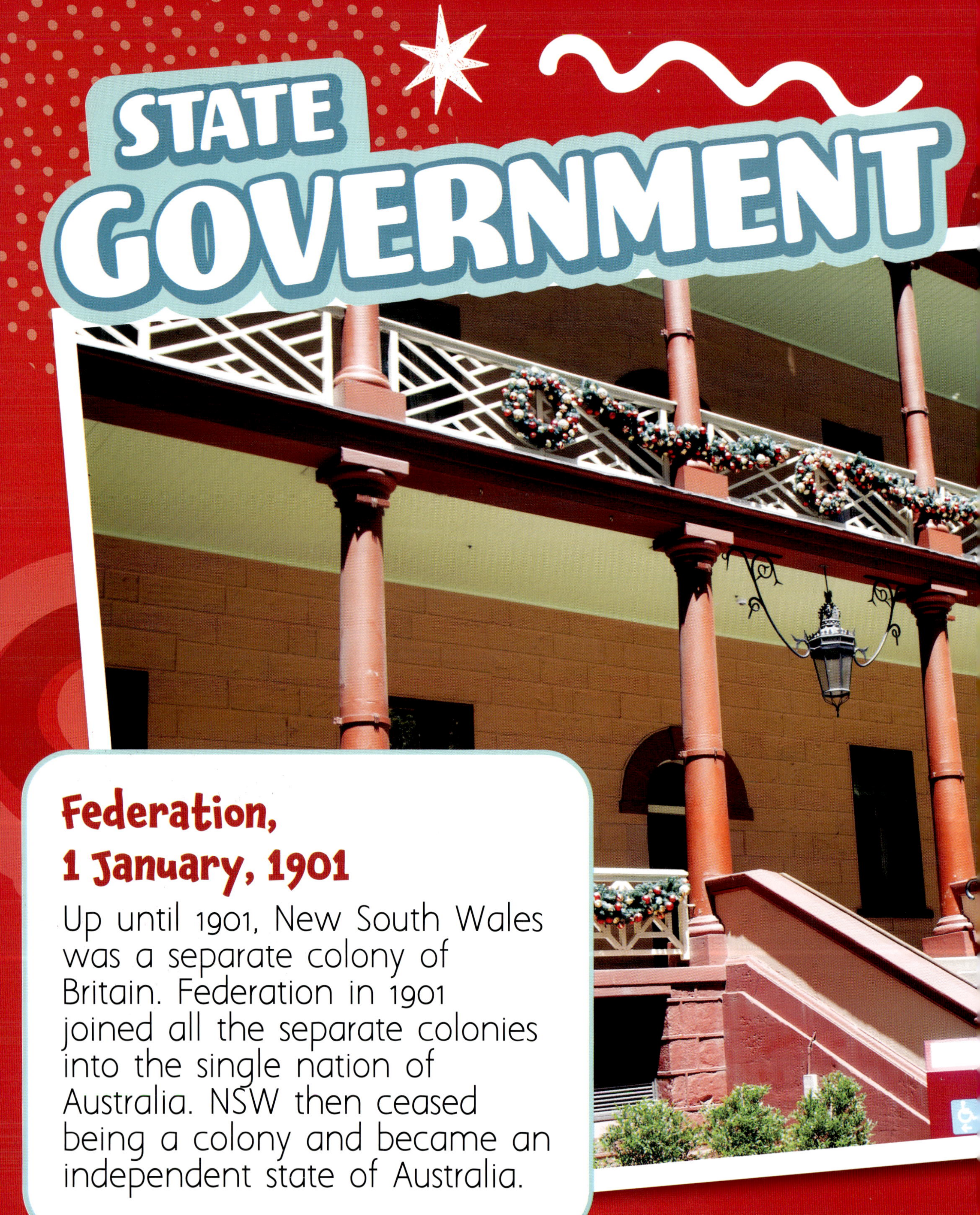

Federation, 1 January, 1901

Up until 1901, New South Wales was a separate colony of Britain. Federation in 1901 joined all the separate colonies into the single nation of Australia. NSW then ceased being a colony and became an independent state of Australia.

The NSW Parliament Today

There are two sections, or Houses, in the NSW Parliament:

The Legislative Assembly - this is also called the Lower House. It has 93 members.

The Legislative Council - this is also called the Upper House. It has 42 members.

The NSW Parliament House is in Sydney. Its oldest part dates from 1816. The oldest surviving government building in NSW is Government House, in Parramatta. Parts of it dates from the 1790s.

All members of Parliament are elected by voters. Laws for NSW are made once both Houses of Parliament agree to them.

NEW SOUTH WALES FLAGS

Australian Aboriginal Flag

The Aboriginal Flag was first flown in 1971. It was designed by elder Harold Thomas in 1970.

What the flag represents:

Yellow Disc	The Sun and yellow ochre
Red	The land
Black	The Aboriginal people of Australia

NSW State Flag

The NSW flag was first used in 1876.

The Union Jack and the lion remind us of the historical connection to Great Britain.

The white badge has four stars that represent the Southern Cross placed on the red cross of St George.

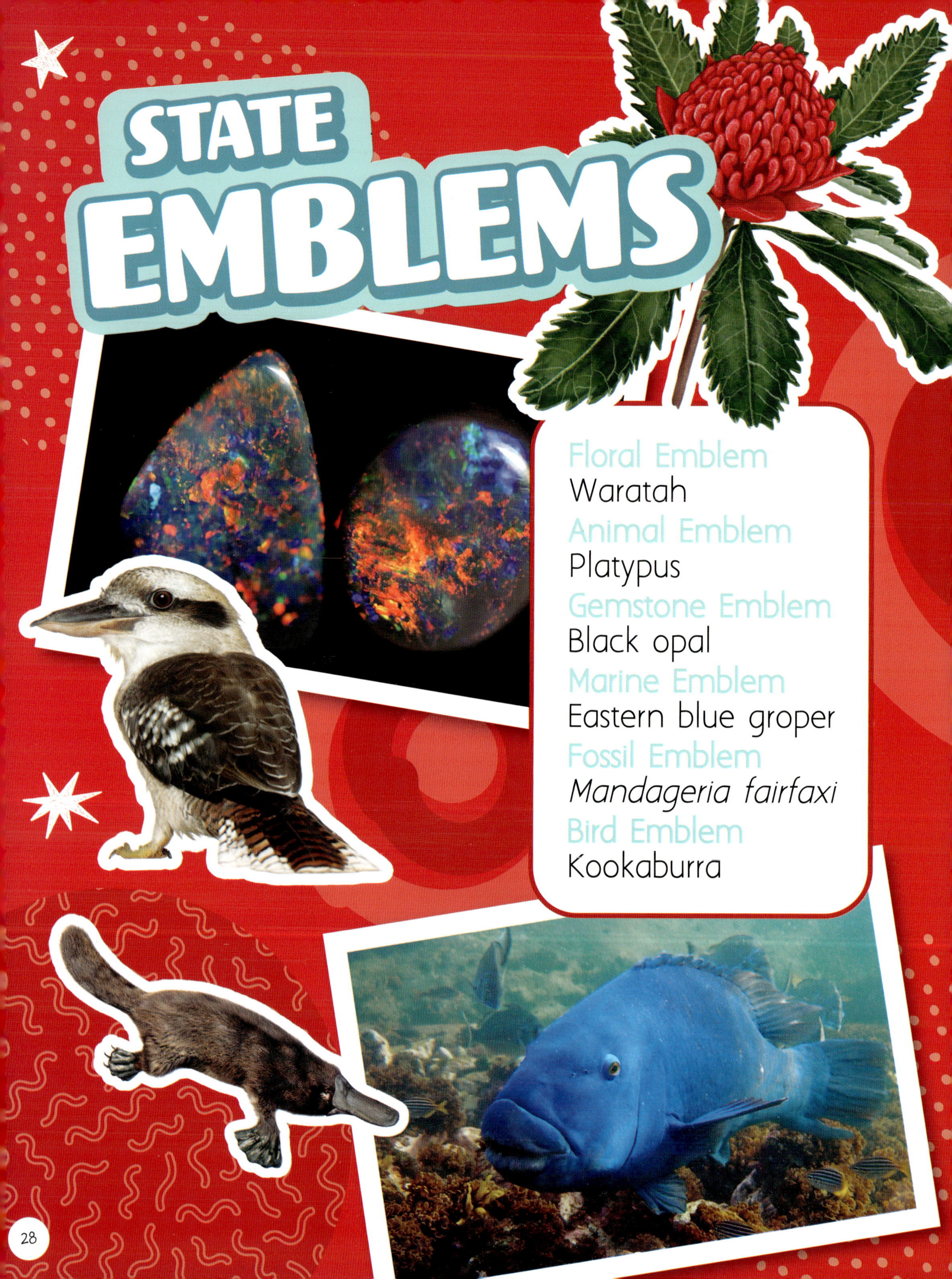

STATE EMBLEMS

Floral Emblem
Waratah

Animal Emblem
Platypus

Gemstone Emblem
Black opal

Marine Emblem
Eastern blue groper

Fossil Emblem
Mandageria fairfaxi

Bird Emblem
Kookaburra

The Coat of Arms

Each part of the Coat of Arms has a meaning:

Crest
The rising Sun represents progress

Kangaroo
Represents Australia

Lion
Represents Britain

Four Stars
Represent the Southern Cross

Golden Fleece
Represents wealth through sheep farming

Wheat
Represents the wheat industry

Motto
Orta recens quam pura nites. These Latin words mean, 'Newly arisen, how brightly you shine'.

Bondi Beach

Sydney Opera House and the Harbour Bridge

Parkes Observatory

Western plains

GLOSSARY

agriculture farming

ancestor person from the past who has descendants alive today

arid having low rainfall

arisen appeared

bores wells

densely thickly

elder highly respected Indigenous Australian

fertile able to grow well

fleece wool from a sheep

greenhouse gas gas in the air that causes global warming

motto phrase that describes ideals of a person or thing

paddle steamer boat powered by a steam engine and big paddles

settler person who goes to another country to live

sparse very spread out

Blue Mountains National Park

INDEX

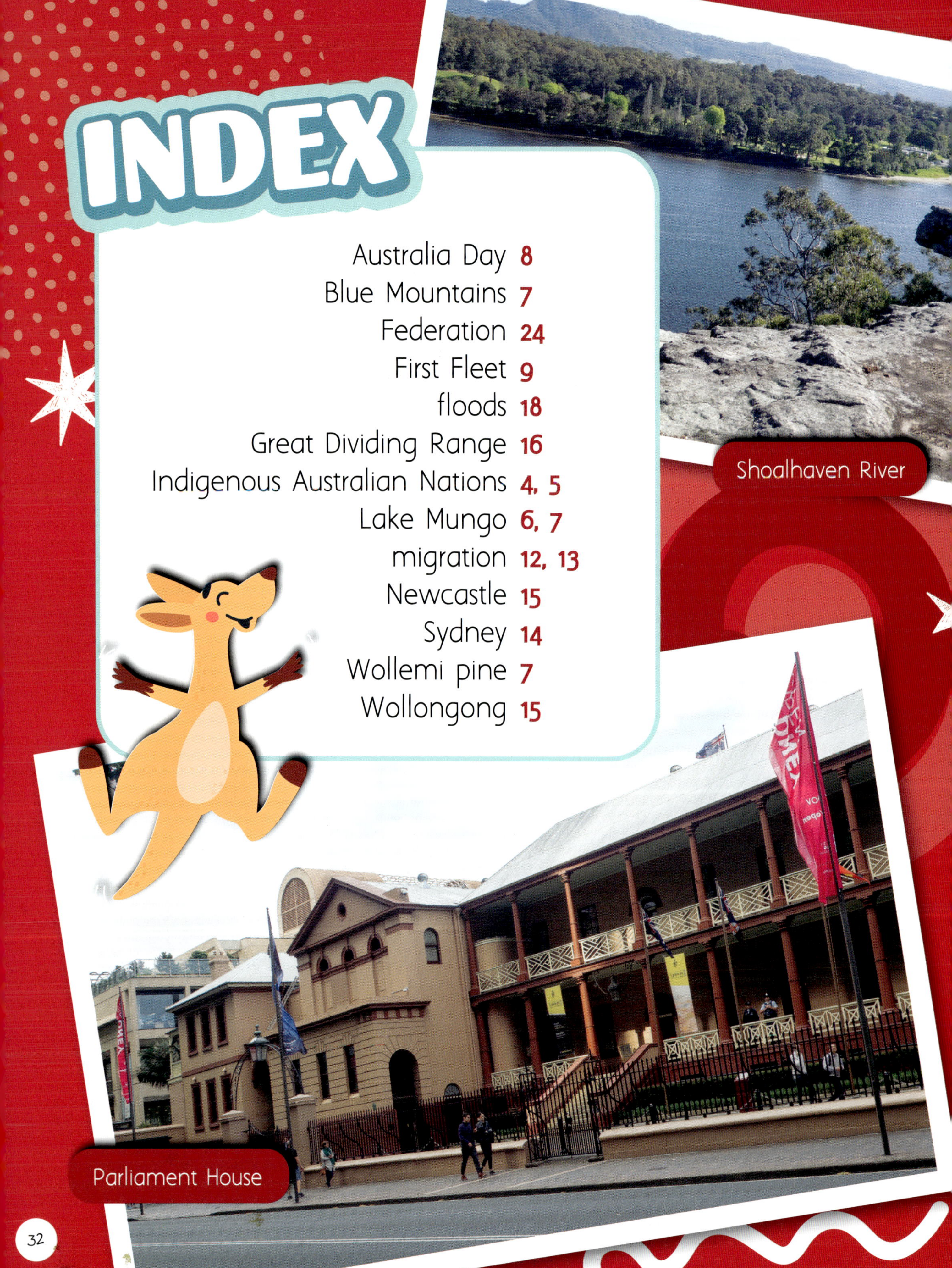

Shoalhaven River

Parliament House

KIDS' GUIDE
TO
AUSTRALIA'S
STATES & TERRITORIES
WA
WESTERN
AUSTRALIA
NT
NORTHERN
TERRITORY